POWER FROM PLANTS

Susan Bullen

Wayland

Other titles in this series include:

Power from the Earth
Power from the Sun
Power from Water
Power from the Wind

Cover: Burning a pile of wood chips to make fuel in Germany.

Designer: David Armitage

Picture acknowledgements
David Bowden 12; Bruce Coleman cover; Environmental Picture Library 6, 11, 24; Energy Technology Support Unit 26; Eye Ubiquitous 9; Geoscience Features 23; Hutchison Library 4, 19, 21, 25; Photri 8, 16; Christine Osborne/Middle East Pictures 10; Topham Picture Library 14, 17; Zefa 7, 13, 22.

First published in 1993 by
Wayland (Publishers) Limited
61 Western Road, Hove,
East Sussex BN3 1JD

British Library Cataloguing in Publication Data
Bullen, Susan
Power from Plants. - (Energy series)
I. Title II. Series
ISBN 07502 0814 7

Typeset by Perspective Marketing Limited

Printed in Italy by G. Canale & C.S.p.A. in Turin

Contents

We need energy

Imagine all the televisions, lights, fridges and cars in the world! They all need energy to make them work. We get this energy by burning fossil fuels like coal, oil and gas. But burning fossil fuels harms the environment.

These cars are using up petrol, which comes from oil.

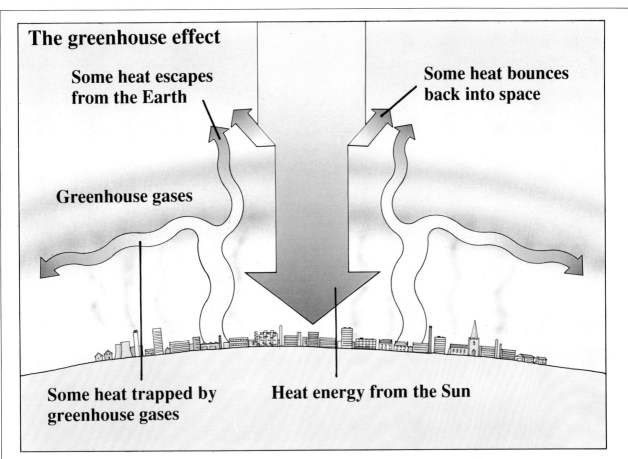

The greenhouse effect

Some heat escapes from the Earth

Some heat bounces back into space

Greenhouse gases

Some heat trapped by greenhouse gases

Heat energy from the Sun

This diagram shows how the greenhouse effect works.

When fossil fuels are burned, gases escape into the air. They stay above the Earth and keep in some heat, like a greenhouse. But if the Earth gets too warm, the ice at the North and South Poles could melt. Then some islands and countries would be flooded. This is called the greenhouse effect.

These trees have lost their needles because of pollution in the air.

Burning fossil fuels causes other problems, too. The smoke pollutes the air with harmful gases. Some of them mix with rainwater and turn it into acid. This acid rain poisons lakes and slowly kills trees.

So when we burn fossil fuels, we pollute the Earth. Also, fossil fuels will not last forever. But we can get energy in other ways - from wind, from water and from the Sun. And we can use living things, like plants.

Look at the pollution from these factory chimneys.

Energy from plants

Lions feed on plant-eating animals.

Plants store energy from the Sun.

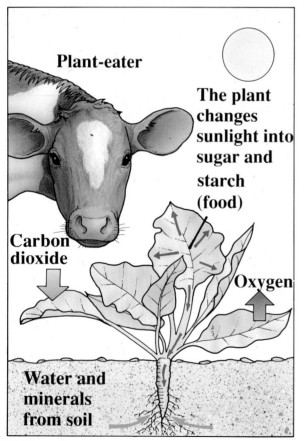

Plant-eater

The plant changes sunlight into sugar and starch (food)

Carbon dioxide

Oxygen

Water and minerals from soil

All living things need energy. Animals and people get their energy from food. Some animals feed on plants - think of cattle and sheep. Others eat plant-eating animals - think of lions and wolves. But the energy itself comes from plants.

A field of sunflowers. Like all green plants, they make energy from the Sun.

Plants get their energy from the Sun. They use the energy in sunlight to help them make food inside their leaves. Then they store this food.

The food gives energy to the plant, or to an animal that eats the plant. But humans can use this plant energy as a fuel.

Plants as fuel

People have used plants to make energy for many thousands of years.

It is easy to make a wood fire. As the wood burns, it gives out heat energy. We use this to keep us warm or to cook food.

These women in India have collected firewood to use as fuel for cooking food.

A Tuareg family in North Africa make tea over a wood fire.
Millions of people still use wood fires. They gather firewood
from trees near their homes.

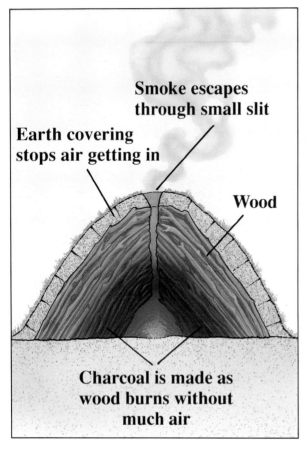

Smoke escapes
through small slit

Earth covering
stops air getting in

Wood

Charcoal is made as
wood burns without
much air

Charcoal is made by burning wood very slowly. Charcoal is a useful fuel. The diagram on the left shows how a covered fire makes charcoal. The wood burns for about three days and then it is charcoal.

This man in China is making charcoal bricks for fuel.

Burning charcoal is hot enough to melt metals.

Charcoal can be burned to heat up kilns for baking pottery. It is hot enough to melt metals for making tools. Charcoal is an important fuel in developing countries.

Wood is just one example of fuel from plants. Straw, sugar-cane and coconut shells are also fuels from plants. When we burn them, we get energy.

When wood burns, it gives out the energy stored by the tree it came from.

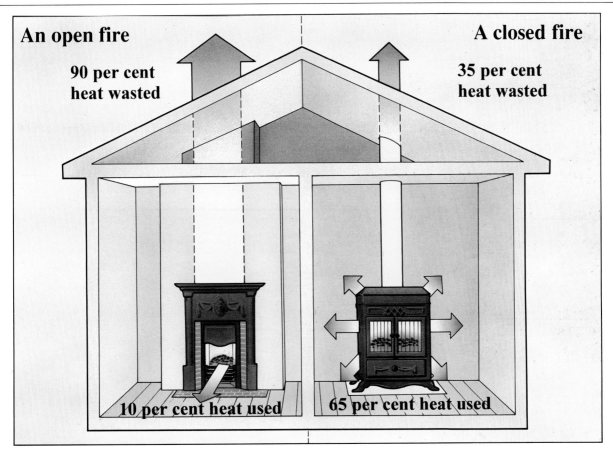

An open fire

90 per cent heat wasted

A closed fire

35 per cent heat wasted

10 per cent heat used

65 per cent heat used

Can you see how an open fire wastes heat? A closed fire burns slowly and saves energy.

A fire needs oxygen to keep the flames going. But an open fire wastes energy because some heat escapes through the chimney. If we make a closed fire, this keeps in most of the heat. Look at the diagram above.

New kinds of fuels

Charcoal is one fuel made from wood. Roasted wood is another fuel. To make this, people chop up logs into small pieces and then roast them in a very hot oven.

Roasted wood burns well and gives out lots of energy.

These men are cutting down trees to use the wood for fuel.

When wood is roasted at the factory, it gives off a gas. The gas can be used to run generators which make electricity.

These wood chips will make roasted wood.

This man has made gas from plant and animal waste.

Making gas from waste

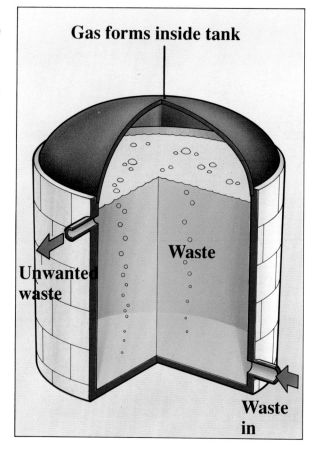

Gas forms inside tank

Unwanted waste

Waste

Waste in

A tank that makes gas from waste.

Today people know how to make gases from waste. Waste means rotting plant and animal matter. As it breaks down, it gives off gases. Some of the gases give energy for people to use.

Gases from waste can be made inside a special tank. Waste or sewage is pumped inside and then gas forms inside the tank. Look at the diagram above.

*Farms often have plenty of animal waste, like cow dung.
Farmers can use this to make gas inside tanks. The gas
provides the farms with energy.*

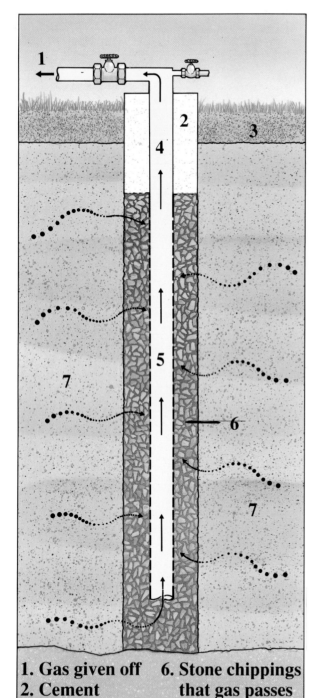

1. Gas given off
2. Cement
3. Covering
4. Pipe
5. Pipe with holes in, to let in gas
6. Stone chippings that gas passes through
7. Waste

Do you know what happens to the waste in your rubbish bin? It is taken to a large dump or landfill site. This is a huge hole in the ground filled with everyone's waste.

When the dump is full of waste, it is covered with earth. Then all the waste begins to rot and gases are made.

Gas forms in a landfill site.

These gases are piped away from the dump.
They can be used to make energy for homes
and factories.

What kinds of waste can you see in this landfill site?

Sugar-cane, sugar beet and seaweed can be turned into liquid fuel. They contain a lot of sugar and the sugar can be fermented into alcohol.

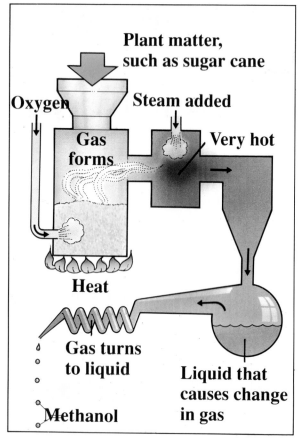

Plant matter, such as sugar cane

Oxygen

Steam added

Gas forms

Very hot

Heat

Gas turns to liquid

Liquid that causes change in gas

Methanol

Alcohol is used as a fuel to run cars in Brazil (above) and the USA. It saves using up petrol, which comes from oil. The world's oil will run out one day.

Left *Making liquid fuel.*

Sugar-cane growing on the island of Martinique in the Caribbean.

We can make fuels from the natural oils inside plants. Sunflowers, oilseed rape and soya plants all contain oil. When the oil is squeezed out, it can be used to run cars and electricity generators.

Energy for tomorrow

Coal, oil and gas will run out one day. Instead we will need to use fuels from plants and from waste. These fuels will never run out.

Making fuel from waste.

This sugar-cane factory in Brazil makes alcohol for use as fuel in cars.

People are using these new fuels in many countries. They are using waste to make valuable energy for factories.

Gas from waste is made in the large tank. Then it is stored in the smaller tank.

It is cheap to make energy from waste.
And this kind of energy does not cause
much pollution. It gives us energy for
our homes and factories. Already some
people's homes are heated only by gas
made from waste.

People have found many ways of getting energy from plants and waste. These fuels are new and exciting. As fossil fuels begin to run out, we will use more energy from plants and from waste. These kinds of energy will help us to live in the future.

The rubbish in our homes can be used to make energy.

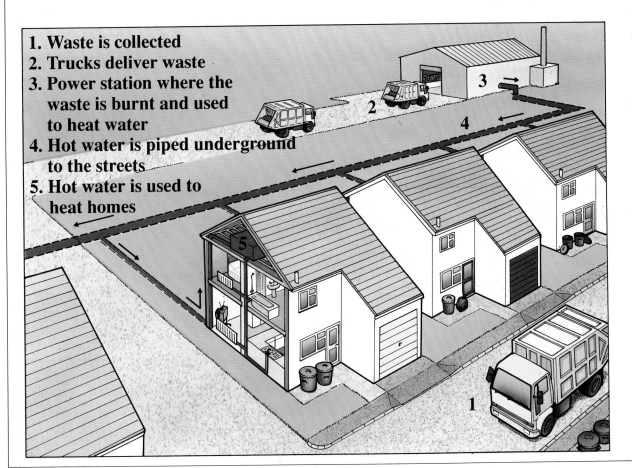

1. **Waste is collected**
2. **Trucks deliver waste**
3. **Power station where the waste is burnt and used to heat water**
4. **Hot water is piped underground to the streets**
5. **Hot water is used to heat homes**

Make a gas-filled balloon

You need

2 tablespoons of dried yeast, 2 tablespoons of sugar, a balloon, a small, plastic soft-drink bottle, a plastic thermometer, some warm water from the tap.

1. Tip the dried yeast and the sugar into the plastic bottle.

2. Pour in the warm water.

3. Cover the top of the bottle with your hand and shake it as hard as you can.

4. Put the balloon over the top of the bottle. Leave it for an hour,

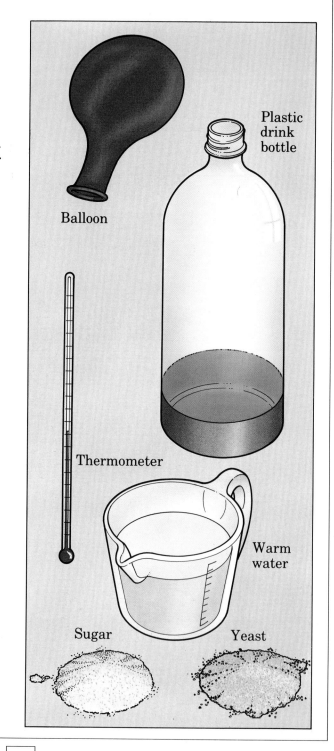

Balloon

Plastic drink bottle

Thermometer

Warm water

Sugar

Yeast

and the balloon will begin to fill up with gas.

5. Try the same experiment with warmer and cooler water. Measure the temperature of the water using the thermometer. Which is quickest at filling up the balloon – cold, warm or hot water?

Where does the gas come from? Well, it is made as the yeast eats away at the sugar. Look back at page 18 to see how people make gas from waste. The gas is formed as the waste is broken down. In this project, you have made gas by using yeast to break down the sugar.

Glossary

Acid rain Rainwater made acid by smoke from power stations and factories.

Developing countries Countries in Africa, Asia and South America. They do not have as many factories, power stations and cars as Europe and North America.

Energy The invisible power that makes machines and animals work.

Environment Everything in the world around us, like animals, plants, rivers, air and the soil.

Fermented This happens when tiny living things called bacteria break down a substance. This gives of a gas.

Fossil fuels Fuels like coal, oil and gas. They are the remains of plants and animals that lived millions of years ago.

Fuel Something that is burnt to give us the energy to run machines.

Gases Light airy substances. There are gases in the air but we cannot see them.

Generators Huge machines that turn energy into electricity.

Greenhouse effect The warming-up of our planet. This could happen if gases above the Earth keep in too much heat.

Kiln A very hot oven used to bake pottery.

Oxygen A gas in the air.

Pollute To make something dirty.

Pollution Something which harms our environment, for example smoke from factory chimneys.

Sewage The waste that comes from sinks and toilets.

Books to read

My Science Book of Electricity by Neil Ardley (Dorling Kindersley, 1991)

My Science Book of Energy by Neil Ardley (Dorling Kindersley, 1992)

Where Does Electricity Come From? by Susan Mayes (Usborne, 1989)

Index